UNICORNS

Cavendish Square

New York

CREATURES OF FANTASY
UNICORNS

BY

KATHRYN HINDS

CAVENDISH SQUARE PUBLISHING · NEW YORK

To Alena

Published in 2014 by Cavendish Square Publishing, LLC
303 Park Avenue South, Suite 1247, New York, NY 10010

LIBRARY OF CONGRESS CATALOGING-IN-PUBLICATION DATA

Hinds, Kathryn, 1962-   Unicorns / Kathryn Hinds.   p. cm.—(Creatures of fantasy)   Includes bibliographical references and index. Summary: "Explores the mythical and historical backgrounds of unicorns including winged horses such as Pegasus, the karkadan of India, the Syrian dajja, the Tibetan windhorse, and the Chinese qilin"—Provided by publisher.   ISBN 978-0-7614-4928-7 (hardcover)— 978-1-62712-055-5 (paperback)—ISBN 978-1-60870-684-5 (ebook)   1. Unicorns.   I. Title.   GR830.U6H56 2013   398.24'54— dc23 2011046274

Editor: Deborah Grahame-Smith   Art Director: Anahid Hamparian   Series Designer: Michael Nelson

Photo research by Debbie Needleman. The photographs in this book are used by permission and through the courtesy of: *Front Cover:* © Jacana/Photo Researchers, Inc. *Back Cover:* Fol.17v How Alexander the Great (356-323BC) Mounted Bucephalus, from the "Histoire du Grand Alexandre' (detail), 1460 (vellum) by French School (15th c.). Musee de la Ville de Paris, Musee du Petit-Palais, France. Giraudon/ The Bridgeman Art Library. *Page i:* © Erich Lessing/Art Resource, NY; *pages ii – iii, 43:* © akg-images/Newscom; *page 6:* © INTERFOTO/ Alamy; *page 8:* © 2003 Charles Walker/Topfoto/The Image Works; *page 10:* Pegasus, the Winged Horse by Fortunino Matania (1881 – 1963). Private Collection/© Look and Learn/The Bridgeman Art Library; *page 13:* Odin (Father Time) flying down to visit the people and distribute money. Private Collection/The Bridgeman Art Library; *page 14:* © Andrew Holt/Photographer's Choice/Getty Images; *page 16:* © Advertising Archive/Courtesy Everett Collection; *page 19:* © Scala/Art Resource, NY; *page 21:* © Mary Evans Picture Library/The Image Works; *page 22:* © Amoret Tanner/Alamy; *page 24:* Courtesy Den Haag, Museum Meermanno-Westreenianum, Hague, Netherlands. MMW, 10 B 25, Folio11v; *page 26:* © The British Library/HIP/The Image Works; *page 29:* Photolibrary/Corbis; *page 30:* © Alinari/ Art Resource, NY; *page 32:* Unicorns on the Banks of the Indus, Hunted by Permission of the King, plate 29 from "Venationes Ferarum, Avium, Pixcium" engraved by Jan Collaert (1566-1628). Private Collection/The Bridgeman Art Library/Getty Images; *page 34:* © akg-images/Rabatti-Domingie/Newscom; *page 35:* (Detail) © Alinari/Art Resource, NY; *page 36:* © Rob Crandall/The Image Works; *page 38:* © Album/Prisa/Newscom; *page 39:* © Jim Batty/Alamy; *page 41:* © Time & Life Pictures/Getty Images; *page 44:* © Vanni/Art Resource, NY; *page 46:* © Werner Forman/HIP/The Image Works; *page 49:* Ms Pers.113 f.49 Genghis Khan (c. 1162 – 1227) in Battle from a book by Rashid-al-Din (1247 – 1318). Gouache by Persian School (14th c.). Bibliotheque Nationale, Paris, France/The Bridgeman Art Library; *pages 50, 53:* © The Natural History Museum, London/The Image Works; *page 52:* © North Wind Picture Archives/Alamy; *page 54:* © Mary Evans Picture Library/Alamy; *page 56:* © Mirrorpix/Newscom.

Printed in the United States of America

Front cover: The unicorn as we typically picture it: a majestic, horned white horse roaming mysterious, magical forests.
Back cover: Alexander the Great astride his unicorn steed, as imagined by a French artist in 1460.
Half-title page: A thirteenth-century unicorn.
Title page: The unicorn takes center stage in a scene of Asian animals painted in 1412 to illustrate a book about the travels of Marco Polo.

CONTENTS

An illustration from a 1491 German book shows a maiden taming a unicorn.

INTRODUCTION

In the CREATURES OF FANTASY series we celebrate the deeds of dragons, unicorns, and their kin. These fabulous beasts have inhabited
the imagination and arts since the beginnings of human history,
immortalized in paintings and sculptures, mythology and literature, movies and video games. Today's blockbuster fantasy novels
and films—*The Chronicles of Narnia, Harry Potter, Lord of the Rings,
Eragon,* and others—have brought new popularity to the denizens
of folklore, myth, and legend. It seems that these creatures of the
imagination have always been with us and, in one way or another,
always will be.

Belief in the fantastic, in wonders, appears to be a lasting part
of the human experience. Even if we no longer believe that dragons and unicorns actually exist, we still like to think about what
the world might be like if they did. We dream and daydream about
them. We make up stories. And as we share those dreams, read
and tell those stories, we not only stir our imaginations, but also
explore some of the deepest hopes and fears of humanity. The
power of the dragon, the purity of the unicorn, the mystery of
the sphinx, the allure of the mermaid—these and more are all
part of our human heritage, the legends of our ancestors still alive
for us today.

MAGICAL HORSES

There were horses . . . white horses rushing by, with white,
shining riders . . . there was a horse without a rider,
and someone caught me up and put me upon him,
and we rode away, with the wind, like the wind. . . .
Then I saw the horses we were on had changed to unicorns.
~W. B. Yeats and Lady Gregory, *The Unicorn from the Stars*, 1908

UNICORNS. WHEN YOU HEAR THE WORD, the first thing you think of is probably a glorious white horse whose forehead sprouts an elegant, spiraling horn of gold, silver, or ivory. This is the magnificent animal we usually see and read about in movies and fantasy novels. It is a shining creature of magic, mystery, and romance. The vision or dream of such a unicorn lifts and empowers the spirit, as a character says in *The Unicorn from the Stars*, a play by the Irish writers William Butler Yeats and Lady Augusta Gregory: "I saw the unicorns. . . . I knew something was going to happen or to be said . . . something that would make my whole life strong and beautiful like the rushing of the unicorns." Unicorns like these are among the many fabulous horses that have long featured in stories all over the world.

Opposite: The unicorn, a symbol of the purified soul, seen in an illustration for the 1937 edition of W. B. Yeats's book *The Vision.*

WINGED STALLIONS

The first-century Roman author Pliny the Elder reported that East Africa was home to "many monstrosities—[including] winged horses armed with horns, called Pegasi." For most ancient Greeks and Romans, though, there was only one Pegasus. This famous winged (but hornless) stallion was the child of the sea god Poseidon and the snake-haired monster Medusa. When the hero Perseus cut off Medusa's head, Pegasus was born from her blood and leaped immediately into the air. "As [Pegasus] glided above the clouds and beneath the stars, the sky was its earth," wrote the Roman poet Ovid.*

Pegasus carried Greek heroes to adventure and glory.

After a number of adventures, Pegasus became the steed of Zeus, the king of the gods. A few other Greek deities also had winged horses. Most famously, ancient artists depicted these marvelous creatures pulling the chariots of the sun god Helios and the moon goddess Selene. Flying horses have appeared in the traditions of other cultures, too. For example, in Thailand there was the winged stallion Tipaka, who belonged to a legendary king named Sison. The most beautiful of all horses, Tipaka was not only able to fly through the heavens, but was also fantastically fast. In fact, all King Sison had to do was tell Tipaka where he wanted to go, and they were there almost before the king was done speaking.

* For more about Pegasus, see *Griffins and Phoenixes*, another book in the CREATURES OF FANTASY series.

Strength and Speed

A myth from the time of the Vikings told of two marvelous horses. One was a stallion named Svadilfari, who had superstrength. He was able to haul so many huge boulders that he helped his owner build a mighty stronghold in a single winter. Svadilfari's son, according to the thirteenth-century Icelandic writer Snorri Sturluson, "was grey and had eight legs, and amongst gods and men that horse is the best." Named Sleipnir, this stallion became the faithful companion of the leading god, Odin. Sleipnir carried Odin through the air and over the sea as easily as over land, and could travel to all the worlds of deities, humans, giants, elves, dwarves, and the dead.

Russian legends praised a remarkable horse named Sivushko, ridden by the knight Il'ya Muromets on his heroic adventures. It was said that Sivushko could leap over a mountain in a single bound, and on flat land his leaps could cover more than thirty miles at a time. Sivushko was easily able to take Il'ya across a huge, treacherous swamp and a wide, raging river when the hero was riding to the rescue of an embattled city. On another occasion Sivushko carried Il'ya two hundred miles in three hours to attack the camp of 40,000 robbers. Sivushko galloped among the robbers with such speed and agility that Il'ya was able to kill every one of them without receiving any injuries himself.

Tibetan mythology has long told of the windhorse. This animal symbolizes the balanced combination of health, life energy, spiritual power, and success. The windhorse never takes a rider on its back; instead it bears a precious jewel that fulfills people's wishes for peace, harmony, and prosperity. With great strength and the ability to run as fast as the wind, the windhorse also carries humanity's prayers from the earth to the heavens. For this reason the prayer flags hung up by many Buddhists in Tibet, Nepal, and India are called windhorses.

Steeds of the Sea

In past times, many people thought they could see the flowing manes of sea horses in the foam of the crashing waves. Perhaps this was why some sea gods were also horse gods. This was true of Poseidon and he, like a number of other sea deities, drove a chariot pulled by horses that were perfectly at home in, on, and under the water.

Sea horses were nearly always stallions, and they had to leave the water to meet female horses. Wang Tai-hai, a thirteenth-century Chinese traveler, wrote, "The Sea Horse frequently comes on shore to seek after its mate. . . . On shore it walks about like other horses . . . and will go several hundred miles in a day." A Persian writer of the same time, al-Qazwini, reported, "The Sea Horse is like unto the horse of the land, but its mane and tail are longer and its color more lustrous and its hoof cleft like that of wild oxen; it does not stand so tall as the horse of the land, although it is somewhat taller than the ass [donkey]." He added that the foal of a sea stallion and a land mare was always extremely beautiful, its dark coat marked with silvery-white spots.

The folklore of Scotland's Hebrides Islands told of yet another kind of sea horse. Called the *biasd na srogaig*, it was a long-legged, awkward-looking creature. Its name meant "the beast of the lowering horn," which reflected its outstanding feature: a single horn growing from the top of its head. And this brings us back to the unicorn.

HEAVENLY HORSES

In Scandinavian mythology, some horses were beings of light that played an important role in the passage of time. Snorri Sturluson explained:

> All-father [Odin] took Night and her son, Day, and gave them two horses and two chariots and put them up in the sky, so that they should ride round the world every twenty-four hours. Night rides first on a horse called Hrímfaxi ["Frosty-mane"], and every morning he bedews the earth with the foam from his bit. Day's horse is called Skinfaxi ["Shining-mane"], and the whole earth and sky are illumined by his mane. . . .
>
> There was a man called Mundilfari who had two children. They were so fair and beautiful that he called one of them Moon and the other, a daughter, Sun. . . . [The deities] took the brother and sister and put them up in the sky. They made Sun drive the horses which drew the chariot of the sun that the gods had made to light the worlds. . . . The horses are called Árvak ["Early-waker"] and Alsvid ["All-strong"].

Above: Father Time rides down from the sky in a nineteenth-century illustration inspired by Scandinavian legends.

ONE-HORNED WONDERS

We are now come to the history of a beast,
whereof diverse people in every age of the world
have made great question,
because of the rare virtues thereof.
~EDWARD TOPSELL,
THE HISTORIE OF FOURE-FOOTED BEASTES, 1607

ALTHOUGH THESE DAYS WE USUALLY THINK of the unicorn as a kind of horse, it hasn't always been entirely horselike. Early writers and artists didn't agree on its exact appearance or even its size. With such a variety of descriptions, some authors deduced that there was more than one kind of unicorn. After all, having a single horn was the only real requirement for being called a unicorn, as the Latin word *unicornis* meant simply "with one horn."

ANCIENT RUMORS

The original source of many unicorn legends was a book written around 400 BCE by a Greek doctor named Ctesias, who lived

Opposite:
This life-size model of a unicorn was created for the 1998 "Myths and Monsters" exhibition at the Natural History Museum in London, England.

at the Persian royal court. To the east of Persia lay India, which the ancient Greeks thought of as a faraway land of marvels. Ctesias probably never visited India, but he heard about and described many of its wonders, including:

> certain wild asses which are as large as horses, and larger. Their bodies are white, their heads dark red, and their eyes dark blue. They have a horn on the forehead which is about a foot and a half in length. The base of this horn . . . is pure white; the upper part is sharp and of a vivid crimson; and the remainder, or middle portion is black. . . . The animal is exceedingly swift and powerful, so that no creature, neither the horse nor any other, can overtake it.

We meet the Indian ass again in a book about animals by the Greek philosopher Aristotle, who was born in 384 BCE. According to Aristotle, "There are some animals that have one horn only, for example the Oryx, whose hoof is cloven, and the Indian ass, whose hoof is solid. These creatures have their horn in the middle of their head." Although that's not very much information, it was enough: Aristotle's works were tremendously influential throughout Europe and the Middle East for hundreds of years. The fact that he said one-horned animals existed was all the proof anyone needed that the unicorn was real—even though one of the animals Aristotle mentioned did not actually fit the basic requirement for being a unicorn. Native to Africa and the Arabian Peninsula, the oryx is an antelope with long, graceful horns—two of them. If you were to see an oryx from the side, however, it could easily look as if there was only one horn.

Roman general and politician Julius Caesar may have been describing another kind of animal seen in profile when he wrote about the forests of Germany in the 50s BCE: "There is an ox, shaped like a stag, from the middle of whose forehead, between the ears, stands forth a single horn, taller and straighter than the horns we know. From its top branches spread out just like open hands." Most Romans probably had little trouble believing this—Caesar was considered a reliable witness, and Germany was thought of as a wild and uncivilized place where almost anything might be lurking in the woods.

Pliny the Elder makes no mention of German unicorns but tells us, "In India . . . the fiercest animal is the monoceros, which in the rest of the body resembles a horse, but in the head a stag, in the feet an elephant, and in the tail a boar, and has a deep bellow, and a single black horn three feet long projecting from the middle of the forehead." The word *monoceros*, often found as an alternate name for the unicorn, was Greek for "one horn." Pliny probably got his unicorn information from an earlier Greek writer, whose works have been lost. Pliny, however, remained one of Europe's most popular authors for a thousand years, and people rarely questioned his writings about the natural world.

Another Roman writer who was long regarded as an authority on animals was Aelian, who died in 235. In his book *On Animals*, he described two different types of unicorn, both from India. One was the same kind of wild ass that Ctesias had written about. In

addition, Aelian discussed the wildlife of the "impassable mountains" that were "in the very heart of the country":

> And in these same regions there is said to exist a one-horned beast which they call *Cartazonus*. It is the size of a full-grown horse, has the mane of a horse, reddish hair, and is very swift of foot. Its feet are, like those of the elephant, not articulated and it has the tail of a pig. Between its eyebrows it has a horn growing out; it is not smooth but has spirals of quite natural growth, and is black in colour. This horn is also said to be exceedingly sharp. And I am told that the creature has the most discordant and powerful voice of all animals. . . . It likes lonely grazing-ground where it roams in solitude, but at the mating season, when it associates with the female, it becomes gentle and the two even graze side by side. Later when the season has passed and the female is pregnant, the male Cartazonus of India reverts to its savage and solitary state. They say that the foals when quite young are taken to the King . . . and exhibit their strength one against another in public shows, but nobody remembers a full-grown animal having been captured.

India and the Middle East

Except for Caesar, with his one-horned German ox, all these ancient writers agreed that India was the unicorn's homeland. So it makes sense now to look at unicorn lore from India and its neighbor Persia. Long before any of this lore was written down, however, one-horned animals were portrayed in art. For example, what seems to be a unicorn appears on a clay seal from the civilization that flourished in northwestern India around four thousand years ago. This animal looks like a combination of a bull, a horse or donkey, and some kind of deer or antelope. A sharp, ringed, curving horn grows out of its forehead.

The creature on the seal is shown in profile, so perhaps it actually has two horns, and one is hidden behind the other. (None of the creature's legs are hidden, though; all four are depicted.) But with a sculpture from Persia, from the 800s BCE, there can be no doubt: It is a little statue of a goat with a single long horn rising from the top of its head. As with the Indian beast, the horn has a gentle curve, although the Indian animal's horn curves toward the front, while the Persian one curves toward the back.

A unicorn seal from the ancient city of Mohenjo Daro, northeast of modern-day Karachi, Pakistan.

The unicorns in ancient Indian literature tend not to be horse-like, goatlike, oxlike, or deerlike. Instead we find several human unicorns, whose stories date back to at least 800 BCE. The plots of all these tales are much the same, but the most famous version is found in the *Mahabharata,* an epic that took its final form in the fourth century. In one episode, there is a young hermit living deep in the forest. He is known as Gazelle Horn because he has a horn growing from his forehead. Gazelle Horn has the power to bring rain, so the king of a country that is suffering from a drought wants to find and capture him.

The king sends his daughter, Nalini, floating down the river on a boat made of leaves. Eventually she reaches the forest where Gazelle Horn lives. Having never seen a girl before, Gazelle Horn is curious and approaches to get a closer look. Nalini invites him onto her boat, gives him wine to drink, and sails away with him back to her father's palace. As soon as they reach the kingdom, rain comes to the dry land. Soon afterward, Nalini marries Gazelle Horn and, we assume, they live happily ever after.

Yet another sort of unicorn was described by a Muslim scientist named al-Biruni, who lived and traveled in northwestern India in the early eleventh century. This creature, called a *karkadan*, was "of the build of a buffalo, has a black, scaly skin, a dewlap hanging down under the chin. . . . The tail is not long. The eyes lie low, farther down the cheek than is the case with all other animals. On the top of the nose there is a single horn which is bent upwards." Modern scholars have no doubt that al-Biruni was talking about the Indian rhinoceros. But readers in his own time and in the following centuries weren't so sure. To a great many of them, the karkadan was not a rhino but an extra-fierce unicorn, and this was also how artists in the Middle East usually portrayed the creature.

In the collection of Arabic stories known as *The Thousand and One Nights* or *Arabian Nights*, the adventurous sailor Sindbad described the karkadan as "a remarkable animal with a great and thick horn, ten cubits [about 15 feet] long, a-middleward its head." The karkadan was so large, strong, and ferocious that it attacked full-grown elephants. When it speared an elephant with its horn, the elephant remained stuck there. The karkadan just ignored it and carried on grazing until the elephant died. Then, however, the elephant's fat melted in the sun and ran down into the karkadan's eyes, blinding the beast.

According to Persian legend, the karkadan loved the singing of doves and would lie calmly listening to them for hours. Humans,

Unlike African rhinos, which have two horns, the Indian rhinoceros is a one-horned animal—so, technically, it does qualify as a unicorn.

on the other hand, tended to enrage it. The fourteenth-century Egyptian scholar al-Damiri wrote that the karkadan "is very hostile to man. When it smells him or hears his voice, it pursues him, and after having reached him, he kills him."

The first (and maybe only) person to tame a karkadan was a teenager named Iskandar. His father had received the karkadan as a gift and proclaimed that he would richly reward anybody who managed to ride it. Lots of men tried, but their attempts at overpowering the karkadan all failed. When Iskandar approached, talking to the great beast with respect and gentleness, it knelt before him and peacefully let him mount. Iskandar went on to ride the karkadan to fame and glory, and together they conquered all the lands from Greece to India. We know Iskandar as Alexander the Great and the karkadan as his faithful horse, Bucephalus—who was sometimes said to be a unicorn.

POWER AND PURITY

The unicorn is irresistible in might and unsubjected to man.

~SAINT BASIL, 4TH CENTURY

WITH ITS STRENGTH AND SWIFTNESS, the unicorn became an appealing symbol of power. In addition, horns had long been emblems of might and leadership in many cultures, so the unicorn's single horn was a good way to represent the absolute authority of rulers. During the Middle Ages (roughly 500 to 1500), many noble and royal families in Europe began to use coats of arms featuring majestic horselike unicorns. At the same time, the unicorn came to symbolize not just worldly power, but spiritual power as well.

MYSTERY BEAST OF THE BIBLE

Several passages in the Hebrew Bible refer to a creature called the *re'em*. This word posed problems for a group of Jewish scholars

Opposite:
The unicorn has represented Scotland in the royal coat of arms of the United Kingdom since the 1600s. (The lion symbolizes England.)

who began translating their scriptures from Hebrew to Greek in the 200s BCE. The re'em was an animal that none of them had ever seen; perhaps they weren't even sure exactly what it was. They decided to translate the Hebrew word as *monoceros*.*

A few centuries later, early Christians adopted the Greek version of the Jewish scriptures as the Old Testament, the first half of the Christian Bible. In the 300s, Saint Jerome translated the Bible into Latin, and *monoceros* became *unicornis*. Jerome's Latin Bible was the holy book of most Christians for well over a thousand years. Eventually, though, people started to publish Bibles in modern languages. In the early 1600s King James I of England and Scotland ordered an official English translation, to be used in all churches in his realm. The King James Version of the Bible became one of the most influential and best-known works in the English language—and in it, the *unicornis* strode onward as the unicorn.

* Modern scholars think *re'em* was the Hebrew name for the aurochs, a huge wild ox that died out in the Middle East long before the ancient translators sat down to their work.

In one famous passage, God speaks from within a whirlwind to teach his servant Job to be humble and trust in his wisdom. After all, God has created many untamable creatures that are far stronger than humans: "Will the unicorn be willing to serve thee, or abide by thy crib? Canst thou bind the unicorn with his band in the furrow? or will he harrow the valleys after thee? Wilt thou trust him, because his strength is great? or wilt thou leave thy labour to him? Wilt thou believe him, that he will bring home thy seed, and gather it into thy barn?" (Job 39:9–12) In other words, it's impossible for a mere human to train a unicorn to help with the farmwork. God, on the other hand, created the powerful unicorn, so he must be unimaginably powerful himself—and it would be a good idea for Job to keep this in mind.

Many of the other references to unicorns in the King James Version emphasize the creature's strength, as well as the magnificence of its horn:

God brought them out of Egypt; he hath as it were the strength of the unicorn. (Numbers 23:22)

His horns are like the horns of unicorns: with them he shall push the people together to the ends of the earth. (Deuteronomy 33:17)

For, lo, thine enemies, O Lord, for, lo, thine enemies shall perish; all the workers of iniquity [evil] shall be scattered. But my horn shalt thou exalt like the horn of the unicorn. (Psalms 92:9–10)

A fifteenth-century Dutch book's illustration of the biblical sixth day of creation. God has just finished making all the wild animals, including the unicorn.

Symbol of the Sacred

For centuries, the fact that the unicorn was in the Bible assured people that unicorns existed as part of God's creation. Artwork showed unicorns in biblical scenes such as the Garden of Eden and Noah's Ark. Choirs sang hymns about the unicorn. Sermons discussed what the symbolism of the unicorn meant—for in early Christianity, and on into the Middle Ages, nearly all animals were thought to symbolize some religious truth or teaching.

It didn't take long for Christian writers to link the unicorn with Jesus. Ambrose of Milan, a leading fourth-century priest, interpreted the biblical unicorn this way: "Who is this unicorn, but God's only son? The only word of God who has been close to God from the beginning! The word, whose horn shall cast down and raise up the nations?" Another churchman of the time, Saint Basil, offered a similar explanation: "Christ is the power of God, therefore he is called the unicorn because the one horn symbolizes one common power with the Father."

Sometimes, though, the unicorn had an opposite symbolic meaning. Saint Basil also wrote, "The Unicorn is evilly inclined toward man. It pursues him and when it catches him up it pierces him with its horn and devours him. Take care then, O Man, to protect thyself from the Unicorn, that is to say from the Devil." The biblical unicorn, Saint Basil realized, was a complex symbol:

> There is also much said . . . about the animal acting like a free man and not submitting to men. It has been observed that the Scripture has used the comparison of the unicorn in both ways, at one time in praise, at another in censure. . . . It seems that on account of the promptness of the animal in repelling attacks it is frequently found representing the baser things, and because of its high horn and freedom it is assigned to represent the better.

Unicorn symbolism continued to grow in importance because of a book called *Physiologus*—Greek for *The Naturalist*. This was a collection of stories about both real and imaginary animals (although all of them were real to readers of the time), with a moral lesson at the end of each tale. *Physiologus* was translated from Greek into Latin during the 400s, and then into at least a dozen more languages over the course of the following centuries. Each translation was a slightly different version, and eventually many of these versions came to be called bestiaries—that is, books of beasts.

Bestiaries solidified the European unicorn's reputation for both wildness and holiness. Here is a selection from a twelfth-century bestiary that gives a typical description of the unicorn and shows how powerful its religious symbolism was:

He is a very small animal like a kid [a young goat], excessively swift, with one horn in the middle of his forehead, and no hunter can catch him. . . .

Our Lord Jesus Christ is also a Unicorn spiritually, about whom it is said: "And he was beloved like the Son of the Unicorns." And in another psalm: "He hath raised up a horn of salvation for us. . . ."

The fact that it has just one horn on its head means what he himself said: "I and the Father are One" (John 10:30). . . .

It is described as a tiny animal on account of the lowliness of his incarnation, as he said himself: "Learn from me, because I am mild and lowly of heart."

It was a common belief that the unicorn, like Jesus, was put on earth to show people how to live virtuously. A thirteenth-century German poet summed up this idea of following the unicorn's example:

The Unicorn has such a nature,
that he has got all purity in him.
So man should also carry on
with all the right purity.

The Mystical Unicorn of Persia

In the Persian religion known as Zoroastrianism, everything in the world is divided into good and evil, or pure and impure, and these forces are constantly fighting against each other. In the ancient scriptures of Zoroastrianism, the unicorn is one of the supreme creatures on the side of goodness and purity. One holy book proclaims, "We worship the Good Mind and the spirits of the Saints and that sacred beast the Unicorn." Another scripture describes a highly symbolic, mystical unicorn:

> Regarding the three-legged ass they say that it stands amid the wide-formed ocean, and its feet are three, eyes six, mouths nine, ears two, and horn one. Body white, food spiritual, and it is righteous. . . . The horn is as it were of pure gold, and hollow. . . . With that horn it will vanquish and dissipate all the vile corruption due to the efforts of noxious creatures. . . . If, O three-legged ass! you were not created for the water, all the water in the sea would have perished from the contamination which the poison of the Evil Spirit brought into its water.

Above: A wall carving from an ancient Persian palace shows a lion attacking a mysterious one-horned beast.

THE MAIĐEN AND THE HUNT

The unicorn . . . for the love it bears to fair maidens forgets its ferocity and wildness; and laying aside all fear it will go up to a seated damsel and go to sleep in her lap, and thus the hunters take it.

~Leonardo da Vinci, *Bestiary*, 1490s

JUST ABOUT EVERYONE WHO WROTE ABOUT unicorns in ancient times and the Middle Ages agreed that these creatures were nearly impossible to catch. According to Aelian, unicorns were too vicious even to get along with each other: "It fights with those of its own kind, and not only do the males fight naturally among themselves but they contend even against the females and push the contest to the death. The animal has great strength of body, and it is armed besides with an unconquerable horn." Julius Solinus, an author who lived about the same time as Aelian, declared, "But the cruellest [of all animals] is the Unicorne, a monster that belloweth horribly. . . . His horn . . . [is] so sharp, that whatsoever he pusheth at, he striketh it through easily. He is never caught alive; killed he may be, but taken [captured] he cannot be."

Hunting unicorns in the manner described by Ctesias was a dangerous pursuit.

How to Catch a Unicorn

Unicorn hunters had little hope of success unless they followed the right method, and even then they were risking their lives. The only way to hunt unicorns, according to Ctesias, was this: "When they take their young to pasture you must surround them with many men and horses. They will not desert their offspring and fight with horn, teeth and heels; and they kill many horses and men. They are themselves brought down by arrows and spears. They cannot be caught alive."

Physiologus, however, came up with a way to catch live unicorns. An early version from Syria explained:

> There is an animal called *dajja*, extremely gentle, which the hunters are unable to capture because of its great strength. . . . But observe the ruse by which the huntsmen take it. They lead forth a young virgin, pure and chaste, to whom, when the animal sees her, he approaches, throwing himself upon her. . . . Then the girl, while sitting quietly, reaches forth her hand and grasps the horn on the animal's brow, and at this point the huntsmen come up and take the beast and go away with him to the king.

The "extremely gentle" dajja must have been a rare sort of unicorn. Luckily, the more typical fierce unicorns could also be lured by innocent young girls:

The unicorn . . . has a single four-foot horn in the middle of its forehead, so sharp and strong that it tosses in the air or impales whatever it attacks. . . . It has such strength that it can be captured by no hunter's ability, but . . . if a virgin girl is set before a unicorn, as the beast approaches, she may open her lap and it will lay its head there with all ferocity put aside, and thus lulled and disarmed it may be captured.

This description was written by Isidore of Seville, who died in 636. One of the most learned Christians of his time, he wrote an encyclopedia that had tremendous authority during the Middle Ages. If Isidore agreed with *Physiologus* that unicorns could be tamed by maidens, then it must be true, and countless bestiaries and other works retold the story.

Most authors believed it took just a single maiden to lure a unicorn out of hiding. But according to Abbess Hildegard of Bingen, the head of a twelfth-century German convent, it was better to send out a group of girls: "The unicorn, you know, wonders when it sees a maiden from afar, that she has no beard, although she has the form of a man. And when two or three maidens are together, it wonders all the more and becomes all the easier to catch while it has its eye fixed on them." This strategy worked best when the girls were highborn and "in the true bloom of youth, for this it loves because it recognizes it as gentle and pleasing."

A twelfth-century Greek author didn't think it was entirely necessary for the unicorn bait to even be a girl. He said that a young man dressed like a maiden would work just as well—so long as his garments were drenched in perfume. As many bestiaries insisted,

pure young girls had a beautiful, sweet smell all their own, and this special scent was the main thing that drew unicorns to them.

Love and the Unicorn

Most bestiaries interpreted the legend of the unicorn and the maiden as a symbolic religious story. The unicorn stood for Jesus, and the maiden was identified with his mother, the Virgin Mary. For example, a ninth-century bestiary said, "As soon as the unicorn sees [the virgin maiden] he springs into her lap and embraces her. Thus he is taken captive and exhibited in the palace of the king. . . . In this way Our Lord Jesus Christ, the spiritual unicorn, descended into the womb of the Virgin and through her took on human flesh." This interpretation often appeared in art, with Mary holding a unicorn in her lap as she listened to the angel Gabriel's announcement that she would become the mother of Jesus.

Maidens surround a unicorn in a fifteenth-century painting depicting the triumph of purity.

Another summary of the religious meaning of the unicorn legend comes from an eleventh-century author named Honorius: "Christ is represented by this beast, His invincible might by its horn. Just as the animal is taken in the Virgin's lap by the hunters, so is He found in human form by those who love him." This was one of the many ways in which love was an important part of unicorn lore.

It was often said that the unicorn laid his head in the maiden's lap out of love for her. Some authors took this idea as inspiration for works about spiritual, religious love, but others were more inspired by earthly, romantic love. The noble French poet-composer Thibaut, Count of Champagne, wrote this song in the thirteenth century:

> The unicorn and I are one:
> He also pauses in amaze
> Before some maiden's magic gaze,
> And, while he wonders, is undone.
> On some dear breast he slumbers deep,
> And Treason slays him in that sleep.
> Just so have ended my life's days;
> So Love and my Lady lay me low.
> My heart will not survive this blow.

The unicorn's wildness is tamed by a gentle maiden in this painting from about 1602.

Another thirteenth-century Frenchman, Richard de Fournival, wrote an entire book called *The Bestiary of Love*. In this bestiary, animals had romantic instead of religious meanings. Here is part of the section on the unicorn:

For this is the nature of the unicorn . . . that no one goes forth against him except a virgin girl. And as soon as he is made aware of her presence by her scent, he kneels humbly before her . . . as if to signify that he would serve her. Therefore wise huntsmen who know his nature set a virgin in his way; he falls asleep in her lap; and while he sleeps the hunters, who would not dare approach him while awake, come up and kill him. Even so has Love dealt cruelly with me. . . . Love, the skilful huntsman, has set in my path a maiden in the odour of whose sweetness I have fallen asleep, and I die the death to which I was doomed.

THE MARVELOUS HORN

On the brow, on the quiet, lucid brow,
the bright horn stood, like a moonlit tower.
~Rainer Maria Rilke, "The Unicorn," 1907

WHETHER THE UNICORN WAS DESCRIBED as horselike, deerlike, oxlike, or goatlike, one outstanding feature marked it as a distinct animal: its horn. And since this horn made the unicorn so special, it's not surprising that people believed the horn itself had special qualities. A sixth-century merchant from Alexandria, Egypt, wrote, "People say he [the unicorn] is completely invincible and that his whole strength lies in his horn. When he knows he is being pursued by many hunters and about to be captured, he leaps up to a clifftop and throws himself down from it, and as he falls he turns himself in such a way that his horn completely cushions the shock and he escapes unharmed."

An even more remarkable horn belonged to a type of unicorn called the *shadhavar*, described in the 1200s by the Persian scientist

Opposite:
Based on a famous tapestry from the early 1500s and handwoven with the same techniques used then, this modern unicorn tapestry now hangs in Scotland's historic Stirling Castle.

al-Qazwini. Hollow, with forty-two branches, the shadhavar's horn produced cheerful, flutelike sounds whenever a breeze blew past it. Other Muslim writers during the Middle Ages described unicorn horns that revealed fantastic designs when they were sliced open lengthwise. The images were white, against a black background, and resembled people, fish, goats, peacocks, trees, and other plants and animals.

The Powers of Alicorn

When modern writers discuss the unicorn's horn, they often refer to it as *alicorn*, from an old Italian word meaning "the horn." As unicorn lore grew and spread over the centuries, alicorn became not just a symbol of strength but also gained a reputation for being able to preserve or improve human health. Most important, it was believed to help people detect, resist, or counteract poisons.

Pieces of alicorn were among the medical supplies kept at the royal palace in Madrid, Spain.

Ctesias, the earliest unicorn authority, wrote, "Those who drink from these horns, made into drinking vessels, are not subject, they say, either to convulsions or the falling sickness [epilepsy]. Indeed, they are immune even to poisons." Aelian agreed, and gave alicorn further power over illness: "From these variegated horns, I am told the Indians drink, and they say that a man who has drunk from this horn is free from incurable diseases." Ctesias said the alicorn cup counteracted poison "if either before or after swallowing such, [the Indians] drink wine, water, or anything else from these beakers." Aelian indicated how this might work: if someone "has previously drunk some deadly stuff, he vomits it up and is restored to health."

Although al-Qazwini mentioned that the horn of the karkadan was used as an antidote to poisons, European writers rarely explored this aspect of the unicorn's powers until fairly late in the Middle Ages. A fourteenth-century Greek version of *Physiologus* included a tale that for some reason did not make it into most European unicorn lore:

> An animal exists which is called Monoceros. In the regions where he lives there is a great lake, and there the animals gather to drink. But before they arrive the serpent goes and spews his poison into the water. Now when the animals notice the poison they dare not drink but wait for the Monoceros. It comes and straightaway goes into the water, makes the sign of the cross with its horn and thus annuls the power of the poison.

Although this particular story may not have spread, the idea of alicorn's effect against poisons did—it was widely accepted knowledge from the 1400s to the 1700s. This was a period when people greatly feared poisoning. Because the causes of disease were not well understood, many illnesses were thought to be the result of poison. Alicorn was such a powerful antidote and so firmly associated with healing that in the 1600s the unicorn became the standard symbol for pharmacies in England and many other European countries.

By this time, people believed that alicorn could not only counteract poisons but also detect them. In 1635 the English writer John Swan described one way this was done: "This horn hath many sovereign virtues, insomuch that being put upon a table furnished with many . . . banqueting dishes, it will quickly descry whether

London's Society of Apothecaries (pharmacists) built this meeting hall in 1672. In the ground-floor "elaboratory," the apothecaries made medicines—many of which no doubt contained unicorn horn.

APOTHECARIES HALL

there be any poison or venom among them, for if there be the horn is presently [immediately] covered with a kind of sweat or dew."

A Precious Commodity

Among nobles, rulers, and high-ranking churchmen—people who might well risk being poisoned by enemies or rivals—alicorns and objects made from them were prized possessions. Whenever possible, aristocrats drank from alicorn cups. These were the ultimate in luxury items: Queen Elizabeth I of England had "one little cup of unicorn's horn, with a cover of gold, set with two pointed diamonds and three pearls."

Most alicorn available in Europe was too slender to make cups out of, so it was used in other ways. A bit of alicorn might be shaped into a spoon used for testing food, or knives and dishes could be inlaid with slices of alicorn. In many places rulers and nobles had servants who touched all the food with a piece of alicorn at the beginning of every meal. In France the ceremony of dipping alicorn into the king's cup lasted right up until the French Revolution in 1789.

The kings of Denmark had a throne made of alicorns that was used in coronation ceremonies from 1671 to 1840. Even before it was made, though, some people knew that the ivory-like material had not come from the heads of unicorns. Its source was actually the male narwhal, an Arctic whale whose upper left tooth grows into a straight, pointed tusk that has spiraling ridges and can be as much as seven feet long. A Danish professor had explained this to a group of merchants in the 1630s, but they had decided to continue selling narwhal tusks as unicorn horns. The alicorn business had been going on for several hundred years and was just too profitable to give up.

Alicorns held honored places in royal treasuries all over Europe. In addition to her unicorn-horn cup, Queen Elizabeth I owned two whole alicorns—one that had been in her family for several generations, and one that was brought to her by Captain Martin Frobisher in 1577. Frobisher explained that he had obtained the alicorn from a "sea unicorn" while he was exploring the Canadian Arctic. Narwhals were often referred to as sea unicorns, and the fact that such creatures existed strengthened many people's belief in unicorns, since ocean animals were thought to be the watery counterparts of land animals.

Important churches also collected alicorns. Saint Mark's Basilica in Venice had three. The spiral ridges had been scraped off one of them, though, so the city's ruling council decreed that all three horns should be "decorated with silver from the points to the silver-gilt handles so that the marks of former scrapings may be concealed, and they are to prohibit any further scrapings except in cases allowed by unanimous vote of the Council." The horns were so valuable that the Venetian authorities wanted to be sure they wouldn't be destroyed by people trying to obtain alicorn powder from them.

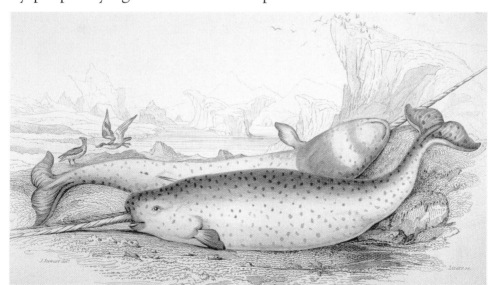

Beached narwhals. The scientific name for these Arctic whales, given to them in 1758, is *Monodon monoceros*—meaning "one-tooth unicorn."

Only the wealthy and powerful could own entire alicorns or decent-sized pieces of alicorn. But the substance had such a widespread reputation as a medicine that everyone wanted it. Alicorn powder, mixed in wine or water, was thought potent enough to cure any illness, even such serious and dreaded diseases as plague and smallpox. Selling alicorn powder was therefore big business. When merchants couldn't get hold of narwhal tusk, they used walrus tusk—and when they couldn't get that, they ground up bones, the horns or antlers of common domestic or wild animals, fossils, and even rocks. Another common cure-all was *eau di licorne*, or alicorn water, which was simply water that had had a piece of alicorn sitting in it for a while before being bottled and sold.

The seventeenth-century English writer Edward Topsell, a firm believer in unicorns, described another alicorn-based medicine and even recommended alicorn mouthwash:

> We drink the substance of this horn, either by itself or with other medicines. I happily sometime made this Sugar of the horn, as they call it, mingling with the same Amber, Ivory dust, leaves of gold, coral, & certain other things, the horn being included in silk, and beaten in the decoction of Raisins and Cinnamon, I cast them in water. . . . The horn of a Unicorn being beaten and boiled in Wine hath a wonderful effect in making the teeth white or clear, the mouth being well cleansed therewith.

MORE UNICORN POWERS

In Chapter 4 we met an authority on unicorns named Abbess Hildegard of Bingen. She not only led a community of nuns, but also composed music, had mystical visions, and was a noted healer. In her book on medicine, however, she never mentioned alicorn—apparently its reputation for special powers was not yet widely known in her time (the 1100s). She did, however, recommend other unicorn parts:

> Pulverise the liver of a unicorn, give this powder in fat prepared with yolk of egg and make a salve, and there will be no leprosy . . . if you often rub it with this salve, except if death overtakes him who has it or God will not heal him. For the liver of this animal has a salutary [healthful] heat and cleanliness in it. . . .
> If you make a girdle [belt] from the hide of the unicorn and gird yourself with it, no plague however severe and no fever will harm you. Also if you make shoes from the hide and wear them, you will always have sound feet, sound legs and sound joints, and also will no pestilence harm you while you are wearing them.

Above: Hildegard of Bingen writing a description of one of her holy visions.

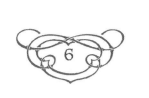

UNICORNS OF EAST ASIA

It is universally acknowledged that the Unicorn

is a supernatural creature of good omen.

~ANONYMOUS CHINESE AUTHOR, 9TH CENTURY

OR MORE THAN A THOUSAND YEARS, MOST Europeans believed the unicorn was an animal as real as the elephant or lion—in fact, many of the real animals in the bestiaries seemed more fantastical to people than unicorns did. In China, however, people always looked upon the unicorn as a more supernatural kind of creature, and this was true in many other parts of Asia. These regions had their own unicorn lore, which was quite different from that of Europe.

THE QILIN

The main type of Chinese unicorn was the *qilin* (also spelled *ki-lin*), known as one of the "four intelligent creatures." The others were the

Opposite:
One of a pair of qilin that guard the entrance to the Hall of Imperial Peace in Beijing's Forbidden City, which for five hundred years was the palace and government center of China's emperors.

45

A qilin embroidered in silk, from the sixteenth or seventeenth century.

dragon, the phoenix, and the tortoise.* All four were spiritual beings and were believed to be auspicious, or lucky—the sight of any of them was a good sign. It was said that the qilin sprang to life in the center of the earth, then went to live in the heavens. Nevertheless, it was the ruler of all the earth's "360 kinds of hairy creatures."

A Chinese author from the ninth century wrote, "This animal does not figure among the domestic animals, nor may one find it in the world; nor does its shape lend itself to classification. . . . Even if one stood in the presence of a Unicorn, it would be hard to be certain that it is one. . . . We know the appearances of dogs, pigs, wolves, and deer. We do not know the shape of the Unicorn." Despite all this, many Chinese writers seem to have had no trouble describing the qilin. They said it had a deer's body, a horse's hooves, an ox's tail, and a long, fleshy horn growing out of its forehead. It was also a colorful beast, combining the sacred colors black, white, red, blue, and yellow.

The qilin's behavior was portrayed this way: "Its call . . . is like a monastery bell. Its pace is regular; it rambles only on selected grounds and after it has examined the locality. It will not live in herds or be accompanied in its movements. It cannot be beguiled into pitfalls, or captured in snares. When the monarch is virtuous, this beast appears." A peaceable and kindly animal, it walked so carefully that blades of grass didn't even bend under its hooves. A qilin could live for a thousand years.

According to ancient records, the qilin first appeared during the reign of the legendary emperor Fu Hsi, almost five thousand years ago.

* For more on the Chinese dragon and phoenix, see *Dragons* and *Griffins and Phoenixes*, two other books in the CREATURES OF FANTASY series.

Fu Hsi, near the end of his life, was sitting by the river trying to figure out a way to record his thoughts and advice for his successors. A qilin came to him, and on its back were eight symbols. Fu Hsi used these symbols to invent writing and also a system of philosophy.

Another legendary early emperor had a minister of justice, Gao Yao, who was aided in his duties by a qilin—or it may have been another kind of unicorn, called a *zhi*, which was a goat with one horn. According to the first-century scholar Wang Chong, "When Gao Yao, administering justice, was doubtful about the guilt of a culprit, he ordered this goat to butt it. It would butt the guilty, but spare the innocent. Accordingly, it was a sage animal born with one horn, a most efficient assistant in judicial proceedings."

The qilin was a truthful, humane creature that usually appeared only when China was led by an especially wise man. The great philosopher Confucius (K'ung-Fu-tzu) was such a man. Before he was born, in 551 BCE, his mother saw a qilin "with the shape of a cow, the scales of a dragon, and a horn on its forehead." The creature brought her a small jade plaque that bore the message, "The son of mountain crystal will rule as a throneless king"—a prophecy of the immense influence her son and his ideas would have on Chinese society for many centuries to come.

Beyond China

In Japanese lore there were two types of unicorn, the *kirin* and the *sin-you*. The kirin was just like the qilin, while the sin-you was a fiercer version of Gao Yao's unicorn. Strong and muscular, the sin-you had a thick mane like a lion's. Due to its keen sense of right and wrong, people asked it to help decide criminal cases. First it sat and stared intently at the accused. If its judgment was "guilty," it ran the person through with its horn.

The Vietnamese version of the qilin was the *kylin*, regarded as a symbol of wisdom and prosperity. It was said that the kylin first appeared in Vietnam in the year 600, when the emperor won a great victory and ended a long period of warfare. To celebrate the land's being at peace, the emperor decreed that the people should hold a yearly unicorn dance. This dance, in which performers wear brightly colored kylin masks, is still a feature of the Vietnamese New Year, or Tet, celebrations.

In Mongolia there was said to be a creature called the *poh*, which looked like a one-horned white horse with a black tail, teeth and claws similar to those of a tiger, and a voice that sounded like a deep drumroll. It was so fierce that it would eat leopards and tigers. It could be a friend to humans, though. According to an ancient Chinese book, a Mongolian kingdom once had a high official named Chung Wa, who was known far and wide for his wisdom and fairness. One day the district he governed was overrun by ferocious animals. All at once, six poh showed up. They attacked, killed, and ate every one of the invading animals, protecting Chung Wa and his people as a reward for his justice and goodness.

Tibetan art often portrayed a type of unicorn called the *bse ru*. A small, gentle deer with a short horn growing between its ears, it was usually shown kneeling beside a wheel that symbolized the Buddhist way of life. European travelers in Tibet wrote about a different type of unicorn, which they said was an actual animal called the *serou* or *tsopo*. It was reported to be reddish-colored and very fierce. The Frenchman Évariste Huc, who visited Tibet in the mid-1840s, stated confidently, "The unicorn, which has long been regarded as a fabulous creature, really exists in Thibet. . . . The inhabitants . . . spoke of it, without attaching to it any greater importance than to the other species of antelopes which abound in their mountains."

Genghis Khan and the Unicorn

In the early 1200s, the warrior-king Genghis Khan united his people, the Mongols, and then launched into the conquest of all of Asia. By 1224, according to legend, he had conquered Tibet and was preparing to invade India. Évariste Huc heard the tale of what happened next and recounted that as Genghis was crossing the mountains between Tibet and India, "he perceived a wild beast approaching him, of the species called serou, which has but one horn on the top of the head. This beast knelt thrice before the monarch, as if to show him respect. Every one being astonished at this event, the monarch exclaimed: '. . . What then can be the meaning of this dumb animal saluting me like a human being?' Having thus spoke, he returned to his country."

A famous book by another traveler, Marco Polo—who had actually lived at the court of Genghis Khan's grandson—told a somewhat different story. The creature, "like a deer, with a head like that of a horse, one horn on its forehead, and green hair on its body," was a *chio-tuan*, a relative of the qilin. It approached Genghis Khan's guards and told them, "It is time for your master to return to his own land." After hearing about this, Genghis sought advice from one of his trusted companions, who explained, "[This creature] appears as a sign that bloodshed is needless at present. . . . Heaven, which has a horror of bloodshed, gives warning through the Chio-tuan." Genghis Khan decided to heed the warning, and he did as the unicorn wished.

Above: A fourteenth-century Persian painting of Genghis Khan (in the gold helmet) leading his warriors in battle.

A REAL CREATURE?

O Unicorn among the cedars,
To whom no magic charm can lead us . . .
~W. H. AUDEN, "NEW YEAR LETTER," 1940

DID UNICORNS EVER REALLY EXIST? Probably not the kind described in the legends we've been reading. But no doubt there have been real animals lurking behind at least some of the stories. And some of these animals might have been older than even the oldest tales. For example, there was a prehistoric creature called Elasmotherium, a kind of giant rhinoceros with a six-foot-long horn. Elasmotherium lived in the grasslands of northern Eurasia and probably went extinct around 10,000 BCE. In later times, however, people may have found the remains of its skull and horn and invented a unicorn story as a way to explain these fossils.

Opposite:
An Elasmotherium on the grasslands of Siberia, as imagined by a twentieth-century artist.

Mistaken Identities

After his visit to Tibet, Évariste Huc was forced to admit, "We have not been fortunate enough to see the unicorn during our travels." The Venetian merchant Marco Polo, who spent the last quarter of the thirteenth century in Asia, was luckier—or was he? Writing about the Indonesian island Sumatra, he said:

After Marco Polo returned to Venice, he wrote a book about his travels in Asia that remained popular for generations.

There are wild elephants in the country, and numerous unicorns, which are very nearly as big. They have hair like that of a buffalo, feet like those of an elephant, and a horn in the middle of the forehead, which is black and very thick. . . . The head resembles that of a wild boar, and they carry it ever bent towards the ground. They delight much to abide in mire and mud. 'Tis a passing ugly beast to look upon, and is not in the least like that which our stories tell of as being caught in the lap of a virgin; in fact, 'tis altogether different from what we fancied.

Clearly, the animal Marco Polo saw was a rhinoceros—which, as we have already observed, was often confused with the legendary unicorn. We've also read how narwhal tusks were passed off as unicorn horns and how the oryx, when viewed in profile, was mistaken for a unicorn. But what about the serou, or tsopo, that Évariste Huc mentioned? After all, the region where it lived—Tibet—was considered part of India by the ancient Greeks and Romans, who generally agreed that India was the unicorn's homeland.

Huc knew of people who had seen a tsopo horn, which "was fifty centimeters [19.7 inches] in length, and . . . terminated in a point. It was almost straight, black, and somewhat flat at the sides. It had fifteen rings, but they were only prominent on one side." As it turns out, this is a perfect description of a chiru horn. The chiru (*serou* is simply another way to spell it) is an antelope-like goat that lives in parts of Tibet. Although the chiru is two-horned, from the side it can look as though it has only one. Moreover, chiru horns—valued for their elegant beauty and their reputation as medicine for diarrhea, infection, and other ailments—were typically sold one at a time, so it might well have seemed that they came from a one-horned animal.

It's likely, then, that the chiru accounts for at least some parts of the unicorn legend. And it shares its pasturelands with the kiang, an animal that has no horns at all but in other ways sounds a lot like the "Indian ass" described by ancient writers. Huc, who observed the kiang during his travels, reported that it

The skull of a chiru, also known as the Tibetan antelope, showing the creature's graceful horns. Hunted for its soft, reddish-brown wool, the chiru is an endangered species.

> is of the size of an ordinary mule; but its form is finer and its movements more graceful and active; its hair, red on the back, grows lighter and lighter down to the belly, where it is almost white. . . . Its neigh is ringing, clear, and sonorous, and its speed so great that no . . . horseman can overtake it. . . . They have never been tamed to domestic purposes. We heard of individuals having been taken quite young . . . but it has always been found impractical to mount them or to get them to carry any burden.

The Russian explorer Nikolai Mikhailovich Przhevalsky, writing in 1876, supplied one more detail, showing how the kiang's behavior could have contributed to the unicorn's reputation for ferocity: "Should one of [the] stallions notice another approaching too near his troop, he rushes to the encounter and tries in every way by kicking and biting to drive him off." So put chiru and kiang together in a mixed herd, and perhaps you've got a recipe for unicorn lore.

Mutant Livestock

In 1825 the great naturalist Georges Cuvier wrote, "Let us not seek in nature further for . . . mythical animals . . . [such as] the cartazon, or wild ass, whose forehead is armed with a long horn." But we've already found some explanations for the unicorn in nature—and there are more. In 2008, a ten-month-old roe deer with a single horn growing between its ears was discovered at a wildlife preserve in Italy. Scientists believe the little deer's unicorned condi-

Georges Cuvier lecturing on prehistoric animals at the natural history museum in Paris.

tion resulted from a natural genetic mutation. And there's no reason why similar mutations can't have occurred from time to time throughout history, turning individual horned or antlered animals into unicorns.

Not only that, but unicorns have been artificially created, and the practice is many centuries old. A French author who visited Africa in 1796 reported that some tribes had a tradition of producing unicorned livestock: "As the horns of the young ox sprout they are trained over the forehead until the points meet. They are then manipulated so as to make them coalesce, and so shoot upwards from the middle of the forehead, like the horn of the fabled unicorn." In 1906 the London zoo welcomed a pair of "unicorn-sheep" that were a gift from the country of Nepal (a neighbor of India and Tibet). Nepal was rather famous for such creatures, which had long been considered a special one-horned breed. In fact they were a type of wild sheep called bharal that, as lambs, went through a process to make them grow a single horn instead of the normal two.

An American doctor named Franklin Dove found these creatures fascinating and decided to try to duplicate the unicorn-making procedure. In 1933 he operated on a day-old bull calf and removed its horn buds, the tissue from which the horns would grow. He then carefully transplanted them, placing one on top of the other, to the middle of the calf's head. In 1936 Dove was pleased to report, "The animal, now two and a half years old, bears upon the forehead the stamp of the once fabulous unicorn. The two buds have coalesced and have formed one exceptionally large and long horn molded into the skull bones of the forehead for support."

More recently, a couple in California performed a similar procedure on a baby white angora goat that they named Lancelot. When he grew up, he had a ten-inch horn growing from the center of his forehead. With his hair trimmed to produce a flowing mane and plumed tail, he looked much like the traditional European unicorn. Lancelot became a star attraction of the Ringling Bros. and Barnum & Bailey Circus in 1980. Many people who saw him were enchanted and felt as though they were part of a fairy tale come to life. Others were nearly as disappointed as Marco Polo was when he saw the Sumatran rhinoceros.

No matter how we might explain or even create unicorns, in some ways they are most real when they live in our imaginations. That is their natural habitat, the place where they can be as fierce, proud, beautiful, and pure as we can envision. The German poet Rainer Maria Rilke understood the unicorn well:

Lancelot, the unicorn goat, in 1981.

Oh, this is the animal that never was.
    They did not know it and, for all of that,
    they loved his neck and posture, and his gait,
clean to the great eyes with their tranquil gaze.
Really it was not. Of their love they made it,
this pure creature.

GLOSSARY

deity A goddess or god.

epic A long poem about the adventures of one or more legendary heroes.

myth A sacred story; a story about divine or semidivine beings.

mythology A traditional story about divine and semidivine beings; myths helped people explain life's mysteries.

naturalist Someone who studies plants, animals, or other aspects of nature.

Scandinavia The northern European countries of Denmark, Sweden, Norway, and Iceland; sometimes Finland is also considered part of Scandinavia.

scriptures Religious writings; holy books.

To Learn More about Unicorns

Books

Dudley, William. *Unicorns*. San Diego: Reference Point Press, 2008.

di Francesco, Mia, ed. *Unicorns: Magical Creatures from Myth and Fiction*. New York: Tangerine Press, 2007.

Hamilton, John. *Unicorns and Other Magical Creatures*. Edina, MN: Abdo Publishing, 2005.

Silverthorne, Elizabeth. *Unicorns*. Detroit: Kidhaven Press, 2008.

Websites

American Museum of Natural History. *Mythic Creatures*. www.amnh.org/exhibitions/past-exhibitions/mythic-creatures

Metropolitan Museum of Art. *The Unicorn Tapestries*. www.metmuseum.org/Collections/search-the-collections/70007568

Owens, Kevin. *All about Unicorns*. www.allaboutunicorns.com/index.php

Parker, Jeannie Thomas. *The Mythic Chinese Unicorn*. www.chinese-unicorn.com

Sharples, Tiffany. "A Brief History of the Unicorn." www.time.com/time/health/article/0,8599,1814227,00.html

Unicorns. www.unicorns.co.za/

Selected Bibliography

Allan, Tony. *The Mythic Bestiary: The Illustrated Guide to the World's Most Fantastical Creatures*. London: Duncan Baird, 2008.

Borges, Jorge Luis. *The Book of Imaginary Beings*. New York: Penguin Books, 2005.

Cavallo, Adolfo Salvatore. *The Unicorn Tapestries at the Metropolitan Museum of Art*. New York: Metropolitan Museum of Art and Harry N. Abrams, 1998.

Cherry, John, ed. *Mythical Beasts*. San Francisco: Pomegranate Artbooks, 1995.

Gould, Charles. *Dragons, Unicorns, and Sea Serpents: A Classic Study of the Evidence for Their Existence*. 1886; rpt. Mineola, NY: Dover, 2002.

Huc, Évariste. *Travels in Tartary, Thibet and China During the Years 1844–5–6*, vol. I. Translated by William Hazlitt. Chicago: Open Court Publishing Company, 1900.

Lavers, Chris. *The Natural History of Unicorns*. New York: William Morrow, 2009.

Megged, Matti. *The Animal That Never Was (In Search of the Unicorn)*. New York: Lumen Books, 1992.

Nigg, Joseph. *The Book of Dragons and Other Mythical Beasts*. Hauppauge, NY: Barron's, 2002.

———. *The Book of Fabulous Beasts: A Treasury of Writings from Ancient Times to the Present*. New York: Oxford University Press, 1999.

———. *Wonder Beasts: Tales and Lore of the Phoenix, the Griffin, the Unicorn, and the Dragon*. Englewood, CO: Libraries Unlimited, 1995.

Rose, Carol. *Giants, Monsters, and Dragons: An Encyclopedia of Folklore, Legend, and Myth*. New York: W. W. Norton, 2000.

Rosen, Brenda. *The Mythical Creatures Bible: The Definitive Guide to Legendary Beings*. New York: Sterling, 2009.

Shepard, Odell. *The Lore of the Unicorn*. 1930; rpt. New York: Avenel Books, 1982.

South, Malcolm, ed. *Mythical and Fabulous Creatures: A Sourcebook and Research Guide*. New York: Peter Bedrick Books, 1988.

Notes on Quotations

Chapter I

p. 9 "There were horses": William Butler Yeats, *The Unicorn from the Stars*, act I, online at www.readbookonline.net/read/26352/62481/

p. 9 "I saw the unicorns trampling": Ibid.

p. 10 "many monstrosities": Pliny the Elder, *Natural History* 8.72, online at http://www.theoi.com/Thaumasios/PegasoiAithiopikoi.html

p. 10 "As it glided": Ovid, Fasti 3.449, online at http://www.theoi.com/Ther/HipposPegasos.html

p. 11 "was grey and had": Snorri Sturluson, *The Prose Edda: Tales from Norse Mythology*, translated by Jean I. Young (Berkeley: University of California Press, 1954), p. 68.

p. 12 "The Sea Horse frequently": Borges, *The Book of Imaginary Beings*, pp. 178–179.

p. 12 "The Sea Horse is like unto": Ibid., p. 178.

p. 12 "the Beast of the Lowering Horn": Rose, *Giants, Monsters and Dragons*, p. 48.

p. 13 "All-father [Odin] took Night": Snorri Sturluson, *The Prose Edda: Tales from Norse Mythology*, translated by Jean I. Young (Berkeley: University of California Press, 1954), p. 38.

Chapter 2

p. 15 "We are now come": Nigg, *The Book of Fabulous Beasts*, p. 276 (spelling modernized).

p. 16 "certain wild asses": Lavers, *The Natural History of Unicorns*, pp. 1–2.

p. 16 "There are some animals": Megged, *The Animal That Never Was*, p. 7.

p. 17 "there is an ox": South, *Mythical and Fabulous Creatures*, p. 10.

p. 17 "In India . . . the fiercest": Lavers, *The Natural History of Unicorns*, pp. 30–31.

p. 18 "impassable mountains" and "in the very heart": Nigg, *The Book of Fabulous Beasts*, p. 78.

p. 18 "And in these same regions": Ibid., pp. 78–79.

p. 20 "of the build": Lavers, *The Natural History of Unicorns*, p. 107.

p. 20 "a remarkable animal": "The Second Voyage of Sindbad the Seaman," from *The Arabian Nights*, translated by Sir Richard Burton, online at www.sacred-texts.com/neu/burt1k1/tale19.htm

p. 21 "is very hostile": Megged, *The Animal That Never Was*, p. 88.

Chapter 3

p. 23 "The unicorn is irresistible": Cherry, *Mythical Beasts*, p. 47.

p. 25 "Will the unicorn": Nigg, *The Book of Fabulous Beasts*, p. 99.

p. 25 "God brought them," "His horns are like," and "For, lo, thine enemies": Ibid., p. 99.

p. 26 "Who is this unicorn": Lavers, *The Natural History of Unicorns*, p. 61.

p. 26–27 "Christ is the power": Cavallo, *The Unicorn Tapestries*, p. 21.

p. 27 "The Unicorn is evilly": Megged, *The Animal That Never Was*, p. 118.

p. 27 "There is also much": Nigg, *The Book of Fabulous Beasts*, p. 109.

p. 28 "He is a very small animal": Cherry, *Mythical Beasts*, pp. 48–49.

p. 28 "The Unicorn has such": Megged, *The Animal That Never Was*, p. 22.

p. 29 "We worship" and "Regarding the three-legged ass": Shepard, *The Lore of the Unicorn*, p. 235.

Chapter 4

p. 31 "The unicorn . . . for the love": South, *Mythical and Fabulous Creatures*, p. 17.

p. 31 "It fights with those": Shepard, *The Lore of the Unicorn*, p. 36.

p. 31 "But the cruellest": Megged, *The Animal That Never Was*, p. 88.

p. 32 "When they take their young": Lavers, *The Natural History of Unicorns*, p. 2.

p. 32 "There is an animal": Shepard, *The Lore of the Unicorn*, p. 49.

p. 33 "The unicorn . . . has a single": *The Etymologies of Isidore of Seville*, translated by Stephen A. Barney et al. (New York: Cambridge University Press, 2006), p. 252.

p. 33 "The unicorn, you know": Lavers, *The Natural History of Unicorns*, p. 101.

p. 33 "in the true bloom": Ibid., p. 101.

p. 34 "As soon as the unicorn": Cavallo, *The Unicorn Tapestries*, p. 23.

p. 34 "Christ is represented": Megged, *The Animal That Never Was*, p. 53.

p. 35 "The unicorn and I": Shepard, *The Lore of the Unicorn*, p. 84.

p. 35 "For this is the nature": Cherry, *Mythical Beasts*, p. 53.

Chapter 5

p. 37 "On the brow": Megged, *The Animal That Never Was*, p. 17.

p. 37 "People say he": Lavers, *The Natural History of Unicorns*, pp. 40–41.

p. 38 "Those who drink": Allan, *The Mythic Bestiary*, p. 100.

p. 38 "From these variegated horns": Cherry, *Mythical Beasts*, p. 46.

p. 38 "if either before or after": Lavers, *The Natural History of Unicorns*, pp. 1–2.

p. 38 "has previously drunk": Nigg, *The Book of Fabulous Beasts*, p. 79.

p. 39 "An animal exists": Lavers, *The Natural History of Unicorns*, pp. 233–234.

p. 39 "This horn hath many": Shepard, *The Lore of the Unicorn*, p. 119 (spelling modernized).

p. 40 "one little cup": Ibid., p. 136.

p. 41 "sea unicorn": Cavallo, *The Unicorn Tapestries*, p. 21.

p. 41 "decorated with silver": Cherry, *Mythical Beasts*, p. 58.

p. 42 "We drink the substance": Nigg, *The Book of Fabulous Beasts*, p. 279.

p. 43 "Pulverise the liver": Lavers, *The Natural History of Unicorns*, pp. 101–102.

Chapter 6

p. 45 "It is universally acknowledged": Borges, *The Book of Imaginary Beings*, p. 203.

p. 45 "four intelligent creatures": Shepard, *The Lore of the Unicorn*, p. 94.

p. 46 "360 kinds": Gould, *Dragons, Unicorns, and Sea Serpents*, p. 351.

p. 46 "This animal does not figure": Borges, *The Book of Imaginary Beings*, pp. 203–204.

p. 46 "Its call . . . is like": Gould, *Dragons, Unicorns, and Sea Serpents*, p. 351.

p. 47 "When Gao Yao": Jeannie Thomas Parker, *Chinese Unicorn: All about the Zhi*,

www.chinese-unicorn.com/qilin/book/contents/1-introduction-to-the-mythic-chinese-unicorn/

p. 47 "with the shape": Borges, *The Book of Imaginary Beings*, p. 202.

p. 47 "The son of mountain crystal": Nigg, *The Book of Dragons and Other Mythical Beasts*, p. 54.

p. 48 "The unicorn, which has long": Huc, *Travels in Tartary, Thibet and China*, pp. 266–267.

p. 49 "he perceived a wild beast": Ibid., p. 268.

p. 49 "like a deer," "It is time," and "[This creature] appears": Borges, *The Book of Imaginary Beings*, p. 203.

Chapter 7

p. 51 "O Unicorn among": Richard Ellman and Robert O'Clair, eds., *The Norton Anthology of Modern Poetry* (New York: W. W. Norton, 1973), p. 743.

p. 52 "We have not been": Huc, *Travels in Tartary, Thibet and China*, p. 267.

p. 52 "There are wild elephants": Nigg, *Wonder Beasts*, p. 81.

p. 53 "was fifty centimeters": Huc, *Travels in Tartary, Thibet and China*, pp. 268–269.

p. 53 "is of the size": Ibid., pp. 125–126.

p. 54 "Should one of [the] stallions": Lavers, *The Natural History of Unicorns*, p. 18.

p. 54 "Let us not seek": Ibid., p. 152.

p. 55 "As the horns": Ibid., p. 197.

p. 55 "unicorn-sheep": Shepard, *The Lore of the Unicorn*, p. 227.

p. 55 "The animal, now two": Lavers, *The Natural History of Unicorns*, p. 207.

p. 56 "Oh, this is the animal": Rainer Maria Rilke, *Sonnets to Orpheus*, translated by C. F. MacIntyre (Berkeley: University of California Press, 1960), p. 63.

Index

About the Author

KATHRYN HINDS grew up near Rochester, New York. She studied music and writing at Barnard College, and went on to do graduate work in comparative literature and medieval studies at the City University of New York. She has written more than forty books for young people, including *Everyday Life in the Roman Empire*, *Everyday Life in the Renaissance*, *Everyday Life in Medieval Europe*, and the books in the series BARBARIANS, LIFE IN THE MEDIEVAL MUSLIM WORLD, LIFE IN ELIZABETHAN ENGLAND, and LIFE IN ANCIENT EGYPT. Kathryn lives in the north Georgia mountains with her husband, their son, and two cats. When she is not reading or writing, she enjoys dancing, gardening, knitting, and taking walks in the woods. Visit Kathryn online at www.kathrynhinds.com